Testimonials

"I have known Bob for decades. He is an ingenuous engineer who has created numerous improvements in his chosen field. It is not surprising that he has managed to create a measurable method to control long putts."

> —Tim Beringer, thirty-nine-year member, Portage Country Club, Akron, Ohio (retired owner and partner, Ceeco Equipment Company)

"Your book will significantly decrease 3-putts and handicaps for the average golfer."

> —Doug Regula, member, Firestone Country Club, Akron, Ohio (retired chairman of the Anesthesia Department, Cleveland Clinic/AGMC, Cleveland, Ohio)

"Finally an analytical system that works not only in practice but can be used during play, and is adaptable to greens of any speed or slope. *Putting by the Numbers* should be a great teaching tool."

> —Mike Beck, member, Firestone Country Club and Portage Country Club, Akron, Ohio (CEO, Polymer Valley Chemicals, Akron, Ohio, and Macon, Georgia)

"I have seen Bob Labbe excel on and around the greens for many years. Most amateur golfers putt by feel. In Bob's approach, the putt must be a well-defined conscious action. The method really works! I wish that he had written his book much earlier."

> —John Halligan, member, Horseshoe Bend Country Club, Roswell, Georgia (retired president and CEO, Amerex, Inc.)

"Bob's method has proven an excellent alternative to chipping. It certainly improved my scoring and I very seldom 3-putt."

> —Ron Kessler, member, Meadowbrook Country Club, Ballwin, Missouri

"It's like having your own putting tutor. This system is for just about any golf skill level. Your ability to read greens and putt more precisely will improve considerably."

> —John Chmielewski, past member of Meadowbrook Country Club, Ballwin, Missouri (CFO, OBAX Infrastructures)

"As a high handicap golfer and terrible chipper, I found Bob Labbe's technique to be a great help to me with my short game. It's an amazing method has worked for me on the green and as far off the green as 25 yards."

> —Gary Halls, Bogey Hills Country Club and Meadowbrook Country Club, Ballwin, Missouri. (CEO, Halls Sales and Marketing)

PUTTING
BY THE
NUMBERS

A Quantitative Method of Lag Putting

Bob Labbe *with* Mike Shaw

ARCHWAY
PUBLISHING

Archway Publishing books may be ordered through booksellers or by contacting:

Archway Publishing
1663 Liberty Drive
Bloomington, IN 47403
www.archwaypublishing.com
844-669-3957

Graphics by Dennis Waldroup.

ISBN: 978-1-6657-1736-6 (sc)
ISBN: 978-1-6657-1737-3 (e)

Library of Congress Control Number: 2022905856

Print information available on the last page.

Archway Publishing rev. date: 3/30/2022

CONTENTS

PREFACE

THIS BOOK HAS BEEN OVER TWO DECADES IN THE MAKING largely due to the fact that I had to be absolutely sure that what I put in print is a system golfers of all skill levels can employ to improve their scoring by improving their lag putting.

The old adage "necessity is the mother of invention" could never have been truer than it was for me. I simply had to improve my long-distance or lag putting to score at a personally satisfying level. The resulting research, development, and application proved the solution. My system of quantitative putting really worked, and as I shared it with others, I saw it work for them as well. Based on those experiences—and at my advocates' urging—I decided it was time to share quantitative putting with the golf community at large.

I am an engineer, but like all good engineering, the complexity of quantitative putting is in the making, not the using. The concepts this method is based on are well founded in science and engineering, but none of that knowledge is required to use it effectively. As a golfer, I knew the method had to be simple to execute while playing, or it would be of little value. And it is: an easy-to-use, reliable, accurate, repeatable way to lower your golf score.

The only requirement to use quantitative putting is the ability to do simple arithmetic in your head. If you can do that and are not satisfied with your lag putting, this book is for you.

Putting by the Numbers is accompanied by thirty-minute practice videos (twenty minutes on-course and ten minutes in-home-Go to: www.puttingbythenumbers.com/tutorials). They are designed to help you visualize how the system works. To recall another old adage, "a picture is worth a thousand words," and a video is even more valuable.

Once you see how easy this system is to implement and the results you get by doing so, you will be on your way to scoring lower on every course you play. However, please recognize that just like learning how to properly grip a golf club, this method requires some effort and practice to produce results. A few weeks of practice will reveal if quantitative putting is right for you.

Over the years, this system has allowed me to reduce my score by 8 to 12 strokes per 18-hole round. I hope you are able to achieve the same or even better results.

ACKNOWLEDGMENTS

OVER TWO DECADES AGO, WHEN, I BEGAN DEVELOPING AND using this quantitative method of lag putting, I would stroke the same putt more than once each time to ensure that what I was attempting to do was repeatable and accurate. This I'd do only when playing golf with my wife, Loyce, and for her willingness, patience, understanding, and participation in developing quantitative putting, I am deeply grateful.

I am also grateful to my golf friends, competitors, and associates for their endorsement of this method of putting as something they can attest to as lowering their scores and increasing their enjoyment of the great game of golf.

Finally, I dedicate this book to the recreational, amateur, and professional golfers who will take an interest in *Putting by the Numbers*, watch my on-course and in-home videos, and find quantitative putting worthy of including in their approach to the mastery of this challenging game.

INTRODUCTION

A FEW YEARS AGO, I WAS WATCHING A PGA GOLF TOURNA-
ment on television, and Johnny Miller was commentating. He
noted that Bryson DeChambeau had a putt of nearly ninety
feet on an undulating green. He commented that it was a difficult putt as there was "no book to tell you how hard to hit the
ball." I hope that by the time you read this book and watch the
accompanying videos, you will conclude that Johnny Miller's
observation is no longer accurate.

The quantitative method of lag putting as described and
defined in *Putting by the Numbers* is applicable to all players
at all levels of the game of golf. This method represents a
means of striking the golf ball in and around the green with
the desired force to get the ball inside five feet, three feet,
or in the hole, depending on how far you are from the hole
when you initiate the lag putt. The promise of this book is
to nearly eliminate the dreaded 3- and 4-putt that destroys
scoring in any round of golf. Quantitative putting is, in es-
sence, a method of striking the ball in a way that enables

you to either make a long putt or get it close enough for a makeable 2-putt.

Terminology key to understanding quantitative putting and achieving the desired results includes individual power factor, putter distance retraction, force as applied to the ball by the putter, and the frictional resistance of the surfaces: greens, fringes, fairways, and cuts of rough the ball travels over on its way to the hole.

I think you will agree that the putter is by far the most important club in your bag. I believe that the quantitative method of putting as explained here in *Putting by the Numbers* will help you substantially improve your performance with that club and enhance your enjoyment of the great game of golf as you negotiate your home course and those you play as you take your game on the road.

CHAPTER 1

WHY

A SIMPLE QUANTITATIVE
ANALYSIS OF THE GAME OF GOLF

GOLF CAN BE TRACED BACK TO THE TIME OF JULIUS CAESAR and the Roman Empire, though the modern game is more akin to what is usually considered its actual origin in mid-fifteenth-century Scotland. Today's game reflects the influence of the Royal and Ancient (R&A) of St. Andrews, Scotland, the United States Golf Association (USGA), and other professional and amateur golf associations around the world.

The game's development and storied history are marked by the names of its most noted and notable players, starting with its nineteenth-century pioneer, St. Andrews's "Old" Tom Morris, and furthered in the twentieth century by Bobby Jones,

Sam Sneed, Ben Hogan, Arnold Palmer, and Jack Nicklaus, who many consider the best player ever. Today, with the current game ushered in by Tiger Woods and Phil Mickelson, the focus on equipment technology and physical fitness is producing a host of long hitters with finely tuned short games, vying for the notoriety of their idols.

Many in the past considered golf a game for the upwardly mobile and affluent, as it was slow, nonathletic, and boring. Today's game is anything but. Golf provides a unique setting where people measure their abilities relative to their skill levels in a self-telling, honorable fashion. The game is a forum for determining your quality, character, honor, and perseverance under adverse conditions in a one-on-one battle with yourself. Golf has become enormously popular with people in all walks of life and of all incomes and athletic abilities, and thanks to initiatives like the First Tee, it will continue to spread among all demographics.

Most people who didn't take up the game early in their lives, including me, started playing by going to a golf range and seeing how well—or far—we could hit the ball using our natural athletic ability. We discovered that hitting a golf ball is not such an easy thing to do. When I was young, I didn't think I had the time or money to play the game. But looking back, I realize I missed many good years with the game, as well as the experience of both frustration with poor performance and the sense of accomplishment that comes with playing well.

The way recreational golfers look at the game is often flawed. If we are playing well through the first three or four holes, we tend to get ahead of ourselves, imagining how well we might score if we continue our good play. This is a formula for disaster. One of the primary goals for professionals early in a round is to get their long-distance putting accurate so that their short-distance putts are not going to be more than five feet. It is, of course, much easier to estimate travel and direction when striking the ball from inside five feet than outside twenty feet.

Recreational golfers are not usually as focused on putting or on analyzing putting opportunities. We focus more on the tee shot and approach shots because we believe, mistakenly, that these are most important to scoring. Of the approximately 30 million recreational and amateur golfers in the United States, fewer than half score under a hundred strokes per eighteen-hole round, according to the USGA and the R&A. For those and even most players who score better, a round with no 3- or 4-putts is only a dream.

Let's break the game down. We know we are going to hit eighteen tee shots. If our putting is limited to two putts per hole or thirty-six putts per round, we have just eighteen shots to arrive at the greens if we are going to play a regulation par round on a par-72 golf course. Eight of those shots occur on the par-5s, and ten on the par-4s. Even on the PGA Tour, it is rare for a player to hit 100 percent of the greens or even fairways in regulation. Still, when you look at a round in regulation from the perspective of arithmetic, thirty-six putts represent 50 percent of the game. Do you know anyone who practices putting half of his or her practice time?

At the PGA Professional Golf Schools of America, which I attended when I first started playing golf in 1996, I learned that the pros' objective is to limit their putting to twenty-eight strokes per round. They consider that an achievable goal.

In this book, I will focus on the quantification of force applied to a putted golf ball and the frictional resistance attributed to the surface upon which the ball is being putted. As I began thinking about this quantitative method of putting more than twenty-five years ago, it made sense that we could quantify our putting as we do the other clubs in our bag. Don't we all assess our clubs in terms of how far we can hit each one when we execute our swing well?

I know that if I hit each club in my bag properly, I get the results shown in the following table.

Club	Distance in yards
Driver	225–250
3-metal	190–210
7-metal	175–190
9-metal	165–180

3-iron	170–185
5-iron	155–175
6-iron	145–155
7-iron	135–145
8-iron	125–135
9-iron	115–125
Pitching wedge	105–115
Sand wedge	90–105
Lob wedge	75–90

The quantitative method of putting asserts that the way we gauge how we strike the golf ball with the other thirteen clubs in our bag should be applicable to how we strike the ball with our putter.

The following chart, developed by Brent Kelley, a veteran sports journalist and golf expert, shows yardage averages by club for recreational and amateur golfers, both male and female. The ranges vary substantially for short hitters, medium hitters, and long hitters. (There are, of course, people who hit their clubs longer, just as there are people who hit them shorter, than these ranges.)

Club	Women	Men
Driver	150-175-200	200-230-260
3-wood	125-150-180	180-215-235
5-wood	105-135-170	170-195-210
2-iron	105-135-170	170-195-210
3-iron	100-125-160	160-180-200

4-iron	90-120-150	150-170-185
5-iron	80-110-140	140-160-170
6-iron	70-100-130	130-150-160
7-iron	65-90-120	120-140-150
8-iron	60-80-110	110-130-140
9-iron	55-70-95	95-115-130
PW	50-60-80	80-105-120
SW	40-50-60	60-80-100

What about the fourteenth club? Why don't we gauge the putter like we do every other club in our bag? Is it possible that the ball's travel distance off the face of a putter could be equal or proportional to the number of inches the putter is retracted from the ball before striking it? The concept, I thought, which is analogous to how we gauge our other clubs, could set us on our way to a viable solution for ensuring accurate lag putts. Virtually all of us have a method for gauging how far we hit the ball with each of the clubs in our bag. The putter is different from the rest of our clubs only in the way we determine distance, which, in a proper putting stroke, is by how far we retract the club before striking the ball.

To further clarify how we use the putter to determine the distance our ball travels, let's consider that all our club distance ranges are based on delivering a full swing. So my club selection for the distance I need the ball to travel is based on my normal swing tempo and speed. I have tried the concept of hitting an easy 7 or a hard 7, and generally the effort to shorten the distance by swinging easier or to lengthen the distance with a harder swing doesn't work out very well. I remember Louis Oosthuizen saying in one of his PGA Tour interviews that the biggest mistake recreational golfers make is not selecting enough club for the shot. His message: when in doubt, take the longer club.

By analyzing the application and use of the other clubs in my bag, I have continued to upgrade and improve the quantitative method of putting. Some years ago, I was playing golf with a friend and business associate, Vince Beringer. I was not having a particularly good day with any part of my game, except for the putting. I noted how effective Vince was in executing his short game around the green. He was using a lob wedge, a club I had used only on occasion and without much success. I further noted that he was executing his lob wedge shots with varying degrees of partial swings. I thought that might be key to creating accurate distance control with short clubs around the green. Today, I use all three of my wedges effectively and accurately by hitting my shots with full, three-quarter, or half swings. Hitting these partial shots with my normal swing tempo and speed has provided the following results:

SWING PERCENTAGE	100%	75%	50%
BALL TRAVEL DISTANCE IN YARDS			
PITCHING WEDGE	105-115	70-75	50-55
SAND WEDGE	90-105	55-60	40-45
LOB WEDGE	75-90	40-45	25-30

The concept of gauging short clubs with full or partial swings is analogous to quantitative putting, the difference being that the backswing with wedges is a circular path, whereas the putter retraction route is close to a straight path. Using my short clubs with predetermined full and partial swing calibration validated my thinking about the value of quantitative putting.

A great deal of analysis has been spent on how long we hit thirteen of the fourteen clubs in our golf bag, but little has been dedicated to how far we hit our putter. One might argue that in an eighteen-hole round, depending on how comfortable we are off the tee with our driver or 3-wood, we could use those two clubs as much as 25 percent of the time. The remaining eleven clubs might be used for another 25 to 42 percent of the game, and the putter for 33 to 50 percent of our strokes. The breakdown in terms of percentages proves the point: the best way for a golfer to score better is to become an outstanding putter.

The pros furnish more proof. You're not on the Tour if you're not a great ball striker. It's what happens on and around the greens that separate the winners from the also-rans. Think Tiger Woods' chip-in on 16 at the 2005 Masters and Bryson DeChambeau's 95-footer on the final hole of Saturday's round at the 2020 PGA Championship.

We might conclude, then, that the distance a putted ball will travel is directly proportional to the distance the putter is retracted from the ball before striking it. And applying that thinking might very well be the best way to make accurate lag putts. And accurate lag putting could be a key to lower golf scores. I think going over the amount of time and effort we put into gauging all our other golf clubs clearly justifies welcoming the idea of gauging our putter to provide the desired distance control.

FORCE-FRICTION LAG PUTTING AND THE STIMPMETER

Using a putter instead of a short iron or wedge around the green can produce better results, provided there are no obstructions, like sprinkler heads, in the way. I mention this because recreational golfers using irons have more chances to make mistakes over short distances than when we use a putter. How often have we bladed, sculled, or hit our short irons fat?

We can use the putter to significantly reduce the potential for error if we understand the force we need to impart to the ball to travel over the different surfaces in and around the green. This is the whole point of *Putting by the Numbers*. Each surface we talk about, whether it is the putting green, the fringe, the fairway, or the first cut of rough, has its own frictional resistance. By using the quantitative method of putting, you can determine arithmetically how much force should be delivered to get the ball to travel the desired distance.

Shortly after competing in the 1935 US Open at Oakmont, Edward Stimpson, an accomplished amateur golfer from Massachusetts, invented the Stimpmeter as a way to calculate the speed of greens. This method uses the potential energy derived by the golf ball being elevated in a notch on a Stimpmeter and allows it to fall onto the green to determine green speed; it has been used throughout the golf world to determine green speed ever since. For more detail on the Stimpmeter, consult the USGA's "Stimpmeter Instruction Booklet" at www.usga.org/content/dam/usga/pdf/imported/StimpmeterBookletFINAL.pdf.

The Stimpmeter measures the speed of a green based on the frictional resistance of the green surface, which impedes the travel of the golf ball until it comes to rest. Knowing green speed is, of course, key to any approach to putting. For the quantitative method, the Stimpmeter provides a qualitative estimate of the relative speed of greens. I think of the Stimpmeter reading in these terms:

- 4–6: Slow
- 6–8: Moderate
- 8–10: Moderate to fast
- 10–11: Fast for recreational golfers
- 11–13: Fast for professionals

(Note: The accompanying on-course and in-home practice videos demonstrate the use of the Stimpmeter with quantitative putting to determine green speed. Visit: www.puttingbythenumbers.com/tutorials)

Different golf courses have different green speeds, of course, but we should be able to learn all we need to putt successfully on a course after fifteen minutes of practice on the practice green, fringe, fairway, and first cut of rough. It is one of the values of a quantitative method of putting, to be able to play both our home and away courses as green speeds change from day to day and season to season, whether they are slow, moderate, or fast.

Quantitative putting works well because on any course, you'll have a plan on how to make your putts. It allows us to determine the travel distance of the golf ball when applying a given retraction distance of the putter and the resultant force applied to the ball, a known value of how far our ball will travel on any surface where we can reasonably putt the ball.

Interestingly enough, I have used this method to hit the ball from as far as 40 yards off the green. It can be particularly useful for days when we're not hitting our short clubs accurately. With a rangefinder, we can quickly, without slowing the pace of play, determine the total distance off the green and on the green to make a quick arithmetic calculation of how to stroke the putter to get close to the hole.

CHAPTER 2

HOW

EXECUTING QUANTITATIVE PUTTING

To execute the quantitative method of putting, you'll need to do the following:

- Establish your individual power factor (IPF), the distance the golf ball travels per unit of putter retraction using your individualized power by rocking your shoulders and putting through the golf ball (measured as feet of ball travel per inch of putter retraction [ft./in.] or, in the metric system, centimeters of travel per centimeter of retraction [cm/cm]).

- Establish the retraction distance of your putter from the ball before striking through the ball to achieve the desired distance of travel (an arithmetic calculation).

- Be able to visualize increments of 1 to 12 inches (or 1 to 30 centimeters) for putter retraction accuracy.

- Establish your unit striding distance to determine how far your ball is away from the hole (feet per stride or centimeters per stride).

  While *Putting by the Numbers* does not intend to teach you how to putt, only to provide a quantitative method and plan to use when you are putting, let's consider a standard procedure prior to executing a putt:

- See how far the ball is from the cup by stepping it off or using a rangefinder.

- Size up the break by looking at the putt from both the ball side and opposing side of the hole on the line of the putt.

- Look at the putt from the side for changes in elevation—upward and downward slopes.

- Plumb-bob the line of the putt with your putter. (Not all golfers find this method of reading a break useful.)

- For a downhill or uphill putt, imagine how water might flow on that surface.

- Adjust your retraction distance based on elevation change.

It is after evaluating these parameters that I do my arithmetic evaluation to determine the retraction distance I need to make the putt. We'll soon discuss the arithmetic evaluation for several examples of ball position in and around the green. The accompanying videos demonstrate putting on the green, fringe, fairway, and first cut of rough, including a composite putt from the first cut of rough crossing the fairway, fringe, and onto the green, and a slope change putt.

(Note: When you are making a composite putt where you are putting from the first cut of rough, be sure to keep the base of your putter parallel to the ground so the ball does not get airborne, which will likely happen if you strike down on or pinch the ball. If it does, your frictional estimate will be wrong, and the ball will travel farther than your estimate.)

PUTTING TOOLS

The execution of a good putting stroke is the difference between success and failure in lowering your overall score. Creating an accurate, reliable, and reproducible putting stroke takes practice. I recommend that you begin practicing quantitative putting in your home or office. You'll need the following tools (demonstrated in the accompanying videos):

- your favorite putter
- three golf balls
- 12-inch ruler (30 centimeters)
- yard or meter stick
- 25- or 50-ft. tape measure

Optional and useful, but not essential:

- architect's scale
- Stimpmeter
- roll of blue painter's tape
- rangefinder

We use the 12-inch ruler and architect scale for practicing the accurate retraction distance of the putter from the ball. Initially, you should use the ruler to develop the ability to properly estimate the number of inches, from 1 to 12, of retraction. Because it is unlikely that you'll have room in your home for a putting distance that requires more than three inches of retraction, you'll likely need to use your course practice green for longer distances.

When you can accurately visualize the incremental retraction distance and get consistent linear results with all three practice balls, you can use the architect's scale, looking over the triangular edge, to check the accuracy of your retraction distance. When you are satisfied that you no longer need the ruler to visualize your retraction distance, you can use the architect's scale both in home and on practice greens for checking your accuracy.

The purpose of the yard or meter stick is to determine your comfortable and consistent level of stride so you can accurately step off the distance of your putt. As the video shows, my normal casual stride distance is 30 to 32 inches. On the golf course, I stride 36 inches because I find it comfortable and something I can consistently do without any special effort. If you don't find a 1-yard stride comfortable or consistent, I recommend a 30- or 24-inch stride; they make the arithmetic easier when calculating the distance of your ball to the hole. You can use the tape measure to mark off striding increments with the painter's tape on your carpet to develop the stride you are most comfortable with.

(Note: Nothing in this method of evaluating your putt is any more time-consuming than what you would normally do. Actually, I have found this method allows me to play as fast or faster than my friends or competitors because when I come to the green, I have a quantitative plan.)

The last two practice devices I use are the Stimpmeter and rangefinder. The Stimpmeter is useful if you have more than one putting surface to practice on because it will give you the speed of these surfaces on a relative basis. In my home, neither the closely cropped carpet nor the plush carpet has any opposing grain. I get the same answer when rolling the balls from the Stimpmeter notch in both directions.

While I find no direct correlation between the Stimpmeter readings and my ball travel per inch of putter retraction, I do find that at lower Stimpmeter readings, my travel distance is closer to linear, and at higher readings, my travel distance per inch of putter retraction is between one and a half and two times the Stimpmeter reading.

The rangefinder is particularly useful for determining distance quickly and deciding whether to use your putter for balls up to 40 yards off the green.

(Note: The accompanying videos include demonstrations of the use of the Stimpmeter in home and on the course. There are also many Stimpmeter video demonstrations available on YouTube.)

INDIVIDUAL POWER FACTOR

Once you have these tools and understand their purposes, you need to develop your individual power factor. IPF represents the force a particular individual derives by rocking his or her shoulders while retracting the putter a known distance in inches, then striking through the ball. The IPF is measured in either feet per inch or centimeters per centimeter. The best place to establish your IPF is on your home practice surface or surfaces. Generally speaking, you will likely be able to execute this method at home with those 1 to 3 inches of retraction distance.

Using quantitative putting successfully depends on your ability to consistently stroke through the ball by rocking the shoulders and employing the known retraction distance of the putter from the ball. Golfers have their own IPF based upon what is comfortable, normal, and consistent in their putting stroke. The distance the ball travels when using this method is simply your determined IPF for the frictional surface on which you are putting times the retraction distance you remove your putter before striking through the ball.

For example, if you have determined your IPF for the frictional surface on which you are putting is 15 feet per inch of retraction, and you retract the putter 3 inches, the ball will travel 45 feet over a level surface.

Let's see how this plays out employing the in-home and on-course practice videos, starting with the in-home video (See: www.puttingbythenumbers.com/tutorials)

- We take a golf ball and insert it in the Stimpmeter notch and slowly elevate the device until the ball rolls down the tubular surface and travels a distance of 12 feet. We then do the same with the other two balls.

Because the carpet is uniform in construction and the floor is level, each of the three balls travels virtually the same 12 feet of distance. Having practiced frequently on this carpet, I have established my IPF as 11 feet per inch.

⚇ With the carpet marked off with painter's tape every 3 feet to establish both comfortable striding and ball travel distances with 1-, 2-, and 3-inch retractions, I strike each of the three balls to verify the travel distance per inch of retraction is indeed 11 feet per inch. In actual practice, using three balls and having the ball travel between plus or minus two feet of the other two balls mimic the Stimpmeter criteria for establishing green speed.

The overall goal of this putting method is to get the lag putt within a 3- to 5-foot radius of the hole so your probability of making a 2-putt is extremely high. Holing a long lag putt is a happy bonus.

Before recommending quantitative putting to anyone, I had to be sure the method could be employed accurately, consistently, and repeatedly. Over the past twenty-five years, I have played more than fifty golf courses around the world, and I can attest to the fact it meets those criteria. Most interestingly, I found that the method is completely linear. In other words, for each inch of retraction and striking through the ball, the ball travels the same distance per inch, whether you strike the ball with a 3-inch retraction or, say, a 7-inch retraction. That is, if my pre-round practice tells me the travel distance for the green is 10 feet per inch for my IPF, the ball will travel 30 feet with a 3-inch retraction and 70 feet with a 7-inch retraction.

After your in-home practice with the quantitative method of lag putting, it's time to take it to the course. Plan to spend fifteen to twenty minutes on the practice green before a round. The accompanying twenty minute on-course practicing video begins with a demonstration of how to use a Stimpmeter to determine the speed of the greens for a given day of play.

The on-course practice video was filmed on the 25th hole of the 27-hole Robert Trent Jones-designed Legends Country Club golf course in Eureka, Missouri, my home course. First, we tried to locate a part of the green surface as close to level as possible. Using the Stimpmeter with three golf balls, we placed a ball in the notch of the Stimpmeter, raising the tubular instrument until the ball fell from the notch by gravity, rolled onto the green, and traveled a given distance. We then repeated the same procedure with the remaining two balls. Once the three balls traveled their individual distances and the ball in the middle was within two feet of the other two, we used the average travel of all three balls to establish the correct

Stimpmeter reading. We performed the exact same procedure in the opposite direction to again get the average travel distance of the three balls. We averaged the averages for both directions to get the Stimpmeter green speed for that day's play.

After using the Stimpmeter to establish the green speed at 8.4, we putted the same three balls on the same level surface using a 3-inch putter retraction. Note that when we performed the first test of speed of the green, right after we got a Stimpmeter reading of 8.4, we got a reading of 8.0 feet per inch of retraction. The similarity is entirely coincidental. There is some degree of linear correlation between the Stimpmeter at lower readings, but that is generally not true for readings above 8.0.

Using our standard method of putting three balls in each direction and using the average of those readings, we determined we were getting these IPF readings, in feet of travel per inch of retraction:

- green: 8 ft./in.
- fringe: 4 ft./in.
- fairway: 4 ft./in.
- first cut of rough: 2.5 ft./in.

The individual surface friction assessment completed, we stroked a composite putt using all the frictional values we had ascertained during our practice routine. The putt consisted of:

- 2.5 feet of first cut of rough requiring 1 inch of retraction
- 4 feet of fairway requiring 1 inch of retraction
- 6 feet of fringe requiring 1.5 inches of retraction
- 15 feet of green requiring 2 inches of retraction

The total composite putt required a 5.5-inch retraction. One of the 3 putts we made and the other 2 putts were within 3 feet of the hole. We had accomplished our objective.

The last part of the video demonstrates a 32-foot putt with a 15 degree slope rise. The slope of green graph illustrates the approximate retraction distance for various degrees of rise and fall. This graph is dependent upon your personal individual power factor. In this particular instance, I added 2 inches to the retraction of my putter to accommodate the rise and treated the rest of the putt as if it were level. This 32-foot putt with the approximate 15 degree rise required a 4-inch retraction for the level distance and an additional two inches for the upward slope. All three balls ended up within a foot of the cup.

It should be noted that most, but not all, practice green facilities have an overall change of elevation of somewhere between 0 and 10 degrees. Making the proper adjustment for upward or downward slope on the green is determined by your IPF and the degree of slope, which requires you to visualize angular upward and downward slope. But even if you are not absolutely accurate in your assessment, if you have accounted for the slope, more often times than not, your adjustment will leave you within a 3- to 5-foot radius of the hole.

SLOPE OF GREEN

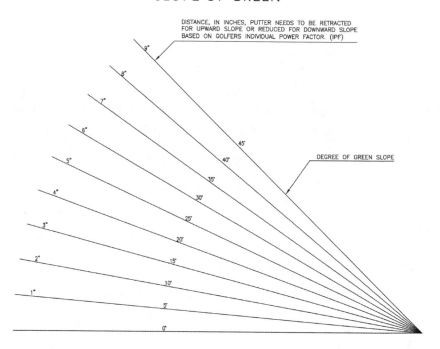

DISTANCE, IN INCHES, PUTTER NEEDS TO BE RETRACTED FOR UPWARD SLOPE OR REDUCED FOR DOWNWARD SLOPE BASED ON GOLFERS INDIVIDUAL POWER FACTOR. (IPF)

DEGREE OF GREEN SLOPE

To summarize, quantitative putting borrows some of the qualitative ideas associated with the Stimpmeter and combines them with the arc radius swing force we use in gauging the other clubs in our bag. We are doing the following:

- ♀ Implementing the friction force concept borrowed from the application of the Stimpmeter. But instead of getting a relative or qualitative value of speed, we are deriving a quantitative value.

- ♀ Gauging our putter, as we do with all our other clubs as described in chapter 1, by establishing our IPF for each frictional surface we are going to putt our ball on during the round.

- ♀ Creating the accuracy of gauging our putter on each frictional surface by striking three balls in each direction on the green, fringe, fairway, and first cut of rough in our pre-play practice, noting the results on our scorecard before we start the round.

- ♀ Quantifying green or surface speed and travel by the force imparted to the ball (IPF) by the putter and the frictional resistance caused by the surface upon which the ball travels.

SITUATIONAL EXAMPLES

So how has does all this play out on the course? Here are a few situational examples from the past few years that demonstrate the effectiveness of quantitative putting. Each round was preceded by a fifteen-minute practice session in and around the green to determine ball travel on the green, fringe, fairway, and first cut of rough.

Example 1: October 2020; Legends Country Club; Eureka, Missouri

Stimpmeter Reading: 8

Ball Travel (feet of travel per inch of putter retraction):

- Green: 12 ft./in.
- Fringe: 6 ft./in.
- Fairway: 6 ft./in.
- First Cut of Rough: 1.5 ft./in.

Situation: My second shot with a 3-wood on the par 5 first hole lands 20 feet from the green. There is an approximate 5 degree upward slope to the green, 20 feet of fairway, 3 feet of fringe, and 25 feet of green to the hole. There are no obstructions to keep me from putting the ball. I go to my putting walk-through procedure, then add up the required retraction distance: fairway, 3.33 inches; fringe: 0.5 inches; green, 2.1 inches; and slope, 1 inch. I conclude a 7-inch retraction is required to properly to execute the putt.

Result: I misread the break a bit, and the ball ends up 3.5 feet beyond the hole. I make the putt for a 1-putt green and a birdie.

Example 2: July 2020; Legends Country Club; Eureka, Missouri

Stimpmeter Reading: 10.5

Ball Travel (feet of travel per inch of putter retraction):

- ♀ Green: 22 ft./in.
- ♀ Fringe: 7 ft./in.
- ♀ Fairway: 7 ft./in.
- ♀ First Cut of Rough: 3 ft./in.

Situation: My second shot with a 6-iron on the par 4 16th hole lands in the first cut of rough in front of the green. The green is undulating to the extent the upward and downward slopes cancel each other out. The ball lies 1.5 feet in the rough with only 2 feet of fringe, no fairway, but 90 feet of green to the hole. There are no obstructions between my ball and the hole, so putting the ball is a reasonable choice. I walk the putt to evaluate the ball travel line, then add up the putt retraction distance required: rough, 0.5 inches; fringe, 0.3 inches; green, 4.1 inches. I figure a 5-inch retraction to execute the putt.

Result: The ball travels on a good line to the hole but comes up 4 feet short. I make the putt and get my par. Canceling the upward and downward slopes appears to be the source of the slight miscalculation. Like all good putters, I don't like to come up short.

Example 3: June 2020; Lake Valley Golf Course; Couples Scramble; Camdenton, Missouri

Stimpmeter Reading: 10

Ball Travel: (feet of travel per inch of putter retraction)

- Green: 20 ft./in.
- Fringe: 7 ft./in.
- Fairway: 7 ft./in.
- First cut of rough: 2.5 ft./in.

Situation: Loyce hits a great drive on the par 4 18th hole, leaving us a 90-yard uphill approach shot. My shot with my pitching wedge is the better of our two but on the back of the green. We are 70 feet from the hole and dealing with a down-hill slope of about 7.5 degrees. The retraction distance is 3.5 inches for distance reduced by 1.5 inches for the downward slope. (See the Slope of Green Graph page 24 for slope of the green in degrees vs. inches of putter retraction; uphill and downhill are the same but in reverse.) I stroke the ball with a 2-inch retraction.

Result: The ball stops 5 feet, 3 inches below the hole, the better of our two efforts. We make the putt for par.

Example 4: June 2019; Meadowbrook Country Club; Ballwin, Missouri

Stimpmeter Reading: 11

Ball Travel: (feet of travel per inch of putter retraction)

- Green: 25 ft./in.
- Fringe: 8 ft./in.
- Fairway: 8 ft./in.
- First cut of rough: 2 ft./in.

Situation: My third shot with a 9-iron from 110 yards ends up 80 feet past the hole on the back of the par-5 2nd hole. I take my putting walk-through and at about 60 feet into the putt observe a ridge to a 5 degree downhill slope. The putt will break left to right with 25 feet/in speed. I calculate hitting the ball to the ridge with a 2.5-inch retraction and letting the 5 degree downward slope (see graph page 24) take the ball to the hole.

Result: The evaluation calculation is right on the money. I make the putt for birdie.

KEY THINGS TO REMEMBER

A few points of emphasis related to quantitative putting:

- ⚑ The ball travel in putting is a friction and force event.
- ⚑ Use whatever putting grip you are comfortable with, but remember to allow your shoulders to create a rocking motion as you putt through the ball.
- ⚑ When executing your stroke, you establish your own distinct IPF.
- ⚑ By evaluating the relative slope, the distance, the green, and the fringe or fairway you may be putting from, you arithmetically determine how far you have to extract your putter from the ball for it to travel the right distance to create the short putt you have practiced enough to make almost all the time.
- ⚑ Quantitative putting takes no more time to execute than any other approach because all approaches should involve evaluating the uphill or downhill slope and viewing the putt from behind the ball and the opposing direction. The difference is that while you are walking and looking, you are doing the arithmetic to tell you how much force you have to apply to overcome the friction associated with your putt.

FACTORS THAT CAN DETRIMENTALLY
IMPACT QUANTITATIVE PUTTING

Using quantitative putting effectively relies on the course greens being the same condition as the practice green. In truth, I have found very few instances over the last twenty-five years of any significant disparity between practice facilities and their courses. However, over the course of an 18-hole round, conditions can produce changes in the putting surface and surrounding areas. Here are some of the most common changes:

- watering the greens, typically done in the hot summer months
- significant wind and hot sun drying out the green and surrounding surfaces
- a soaking rain (You can check the effect out easily enough when you restart a round after a delay by putting a few balls on the level surface of a green.)
- grass growth, especially during high growth months, which can marginally slow the surfaces

Such changes make it advisable to check the green speed every four or five holes to see if it is holding to what you had determined in your pre-round practice.

RULES OF THE GAME

The rules of golf have changed to some extent over the more than twenty years I have been developing content for this book. These current United States Golf Association (USGA) rules apply to quantitative putting:

⚘ Rule 13.1e: No Deliberate Testing of Greens

During a round and while play is stopped under Rule 5.7a, a player must not deliberately take either of these actions to test the putting green or a wrong green:

> Rub the surface, or
> Roll a ball

Exception: **Testing Greens When Between Two Holes**: Between two holes, a player may rub the surface or roll a ball on the putting green of the hole just completed and on any practice green (Rule 5.5b).

⚘ Rule 5.5a No Practice Strokes While Playing Hole

While playing a hole, a player must not make a practice stroke at any ball on or off the course.

⛳ Rule 5.5b: Restriction on Practice Strokes between Two Holes

Between two holes, a player must not make a practice stroke. Exception: The player may practice putting or chipping on or near:

- ⛳ the putting green of the hole just completed and the practice green (see Rule 13.1e)
- ⛳ the teeing area of the next hole

Such practice strokes must not be made from a bunker and must not unreasonably delay play (see Rule 5.6 a). As well, per Committee Procedures, Section 8, Model Rule 1-2, the Committee may adopt a local rule prohibiting practice putting or chipping on or near the putting green of the hole just completed.

⛳ Rule 5.6 Unreasonable Delay of Play

A player must not unreasonably delay play, either when playing a hole or between two holes. A player may be allowed a short delay for certain reasons:

- ⛳ when a player seeks help from a referee or the Committee,
- ⛳ when the player becomes injured or ill, or
- ⛳ when there is another good reason.

Knowing these rules will help you ensure that any practicing putting or chipping you do between holes is legal and acceptable. A complete review of USGA Rules 5 and 13 will help you understand the letter and intent of each.

The rain delays in the third round of the 2021 Masters cost several of the contending players strokes due to the vastly changed speed of greens. They were unable to make timely adjustments to the new conditions. The quantitative method of putting will help you make an adjustment quickly. However, if you miss a putting distance significantly and think you executed the putt according to your measurements, invoke the practice rule, provided you do not slow play.

A 10 percent miss is significant enough to check, particularly if there are condition changes. Playing in June 2020, I observed that the speed of the greens changed from 15 feet per inch of retraction to 18, then to 20 feet over the 18-hole round, due to drying conditions caused by wind and hot sun.

Using the quantitative system of lag putting effectively requires you to understand how your putting IPF is calculated for all surfaces on and around the green. Simply put, if you plan well, even the most accomplished players can use the quantitative method to lower their scores.

CHAPTER 3

WHERE

QUANTITATIVE PUTTING WORKS
HOME AND AWAY ON ALL
DIFFERENT TYPES OF SURFACES

NOW THAT WE HAVE DISCUSSED THE "WHY" AND "HOW" OF quantitative putting, let's talk about where we are working to improve our scores by improving our lag putting.

In general, few recreational golfers hit their approach shots close to the pin. From what I have observed over the years of practicing and playing golf, I estimate four out of five recreational players reach the green with putts longer than 20 feet. The goal of quantitative putting is to get the resulting lag putts within 3 to 5 feet of the cup, so you can 2-putt every green; 2-putting is all about having the confidence and developing the touch-and-feel sense that is quantitatively measurable by practicing retraction distance.

PRACTICE REGIMENS

You can practice quantitative putting wherever the surface allows you to putt. If you live in an area where winter temperatures prevent you from playing, you can practice this method in your house, using carpeted surfaces with 20 to 50 feet of putting distance. Even if you play in compromising weather, you can practice putting by the numbers during the off-months to prepare yourself for spring, when the greens are much better for putting. If you can't play, identify outdoor spaces around your home, office, or lawn with properly cropped grass. These can serve as ideal putting surfaces, artificial or real.

Before each round of golf, on my home course or an unfamiliar course, I spend up to twenty minutes practicing lag putting on the actual putting surface, the fringe, the fairway, and the first cut of rough. Practicing on four different surfaces helps me determine my retraction distance and see how to deliver the ball a certain distance. For example, putting on a fast green, I might find myself using my IPF and retracting 1 inch to yield 20 to 25 feet of ball travel; on the fringe, 7 feet of travel; on the fairway surface, 6 feet; and in the first cut of rough, which is as slow a surface as I recommend trying this method on, only 2 feet of ball travel. Be it a simple putt on the putting surface or a composite putt that incorporates first cut of rough, fairway, fringe, and putting surface, I can quickly determine what it will take to achieve a good outcome.

I believe the most valuable use of time before playing a round of golf is practicing putting on and around the green. During prime playing months, most groomed courses have between a 12- and 24-foot ball travel distance for 1 inch of putter retraction.

I begin my practice routine as follows: I retract my putter 3 inches and strike three balls from the same position on a flat putting surface so I can see the roll on the practice green. After striking the ball, I walk off the distance the ball travels by using my 1-yard-per-step gait. If you have a rangefinder in your possession, you can shoot the flagstick so you don't have to walk off the distances each time. Doing either gives me an idea about the distance my ball travels per inch of retraction.

GREENS AND GRASSES

My experience indicates there is little or no difference in travel distance on different types of greens. However, Bermuda greens, which are typically used in the Southern United States, roll differently based on whether you are putting with or against the grain. If you practice with the grain and then in the opposite direction, you will have an idea of the effects on the ball's travel distance.

I repeat this process as much as I can to determine the average travel distance per inch of retraction. If I'm putting on a Bermuda or Poa Annua practice green, the ball might travel 17 feet per inch with the grain and 16 feet against the grain. I will try other locations on the green to confirm my conclusion about relative speeds.

If I can find another relatively flat surface to verify my findings, I putt the ball both ways, using my calculation of differences between putting with and against the grain to see if I am within a foot of travel each way. This test has proven an accurate way to judge roll more than 95 percent of the time.

On the rare occasion I don't get the results I expect, I retest my IPF using the same test location. Then I make minor adjustments to my calculations to get the best formula to take the course.

Next, I test the speed of the fringe around the green. I find a leveled or flat surface and strike the ball with a 3-inch retraction, checking the travel distance in both directions. That generally proves sufficient to determine the travel for each inch of retraction.

I repeat this procedure on the fairway surface, putting three balls in each direction using a 3-inch retraction to determine travel distance and travel distance per inch of retraction.

Then I repeat this process for the first cut of rough.

Using my IPF, I can usually depend on the following relationship between surface and putter retraction:

- Green surface, Bentgrass: 17 to 22 feet per inch of retraction
- Fringe surface (Zoysia or Bermuda): 6 to 7 feet per inch of retraction
- Fairway surface (Zoysia or Bermuda): 6 to 7 feet per inch of retraction
- First cut of rough (combination of grass and weed species): 2 to 3 feet per inch of retraction
- Second cut of rough (combination of grass and weed species): 1 foot per inch of retraction

Different surfaces have different frictional factors. Measuring as you practice can help you determine the frictional difference between putting surfaces. And you can use the arithmetic calculation to determine the overall potential striking power needed in a composite putt.

I play most of my golf on my home course. But I also enjoy playing other golf courses. I find it valuable and interesting to play away courses with different conditions that cause me to adjust my IPF for the greens, fringes, fairways, and first cut of rough. And it is extremely gratifying and serves to confirm my belief in my system of quantitative putting when I putt an away course at or better than 32 putts per round. Variations don't compromise my belief in my system, as they are normally caused by course conditions. In fact, the changes in condition that can occur during a round of golf make quantitative putting even more useful.

CHAPTER 4

WHEN

PREPARATION AND PRACTICE: KEYS TO SUCCESS

DIFFERENT GOLF COURSES REQUIRE DIFFERENT APPROACHES to putting on their greens, fringes, fairways, and first and second cuts of rough. I try to be in the practice area about thirty to thirty-five minutes before my tee time, first to gauge the putting requirements for the various surfaces, then to warm up with my other clubs. My experience of playing at different courses has shown that the travel distance of a putted ball hit with the same force can vary by up to plus or minus 5 percent.

On most courses, all eighteen greens roll the same. Of course, conditions matter, such as when the greens have been aerated or sanded, or if they are watered or rained on before or during your game. Under these conditions, where it's not possible to go through your practice regimen, you can practice according to USGA Rule 5.5.

When conditions of the greens are other than their usual, I periodically test the speed throughout the round, staying true to Rule 5.5 (and to Rule 5.6a on delays).

The rules call to mind two questions: After you finish playing a hole during a normal round of golf, are you allowed to drop the ball and putt it again for practice? Can you hit short chips to pass the time while waiting on the tee for the fairway ahead to get cleared? According to the Rule 5.5, the answer to both questions is yes, though there are some limitations.

QUANTITATIVE PUTTING AND MY GAME OVER THE YEARS

Since 1996, I have been a member of three golf clubs. It was at Town Lake Country Club in Woodstock, Georgia, that I proved to myself the merits of quantitative putting. The subsequent years of practice and applying it at my clubs and on courses throughout the world have convinced me it will benefit anyone who chooses to adopt it.

Even though I still consider myself an average recreational golfer, my game is on the upswing. It's due to my putting, which, I can confirm, has improved much more than the rest of my game. As I have mentioned, it's nice to have a lot of power off the tee, but it doesn't always translate to better scoring. To post consistently low scores, you have to be a good putter.

Today, I'm using between 28 and 32 putts per 18 holes, my average being slightly above 30.5. According to the calculations at https://mygolfspy.com/mygolfspy-labs-the-arccos-putting-study/, my putting is consistent with players in the 1 to 4 handicap range. Despite my lack of frequent practice, having a reliable, reproducible putting stroke has substantially improved my scoring.

At https://www.myscorecard.com/, you can keep track of your performance on greens as well as other key parts of your game, like fairways and greens reached in regulation. These statistics are crucial to know, as they demonstrate how you are producing your scores and what you can work on to improve.

Virtually all greens have undulations and slope changes that affect your measurements and your expected outcomes. They challenge the confidence of a recreational golfer in terms of the ability to deliver the ball accurately and get close to the cup from distances outside 10 or 20 feet.

Using the quantitative method of putting, you can achieve a new level of confidence, as this method does not rely on touch-and-feel instincts to dictate how far the ball will travel. Through this method, you can compute what it takes to get the ball to the hole accurately and within 3 to 5 feet. It also increases the chance of a 1-putt.

Every golfer knows that confidence is key in making any golf stroke and most important in putting, as it represents as much as half the game. As one of the oldest and most clichéd golf sayings goes, "Drive for show, putt for dough."

In the more than twenty-five years since I started developing this method, whenever I feel that any part of my game is not going well, I know I can always rely on my putting. I have such confidence that when I putt, regardless of the distance, be it 20 feet or 90 feet from the hole, I expect to make it; if I don't, I am disappointed.

I can assure you that if you implement this quantitative method, your putting will improve greatly. You should expect to see your putting strokes reduced by 5 to 10 strokes per round. I am not aware of any other method that can claim such an improvement in a player's game. Even if you're a good putter, examining what you're doing using this quantitative analysis will help you reduce your number of putts per round.

To fully benefit from quantitative putting, you must put some serious time into your practice. You can begin anywhere, such as in your office or home, wherever you have a carpeted surface and enough distance to putt the ball 20 to 50 feet. Once you practice on carpet and have developed some confidence in the reliability of your retraction consistency, you can take it to the course.

The "when" of quantitative putting includes giving yourself fifteen to twenty minutes on the course practice green before teeing off—even if that means you don't have enough time to warm up with your full-swing clubs. That preparation will help you implement the method as you play and employ it effectively.

Remember that putting is up to half the game. A few swings with a wood or iron is usually enough to loosen up and get you comfortable with your longer clubs. Getting your putting right, however, is most important to scoring well.

CHAPTER 5

WHO

THIS BOOK'S FOR YOU

PUTTING BY THE NUMBERS, OR QUANTITATIVE PUTTING, CAN improve the scores of golfers of all skill levels. Players who feel they need to improve their lag putting will find this method will improve their game and lower their scores. Incorporating the method into your game requires only that you can do simple, if quick, arithmetic—addition, subtraction, multiplication, and division—visualize your retraction in terms of inches, step off or otherwise measure your putting distances, and read the grades of an upward or downward slope.

PRE-ROUND PRACTICE PUTTING

I cannot overstate the importance of practicing fifteen to twenty minutes before your round. I make sure that I practice at least fifteen minutes to get an idea about the surface and how it can affect my game.

First, I look for a flat surface, as flat as I can find at the green, and make sure it is at least 60 feet long. If you can find a flat green surface longer than 60 feet, that's even better, but you need at least 60 feet of green to practice effectively.

In the accompanying on-course video (Go to: www.puttingbythenumbers.com/tutorials), you will see that the flat surface I find measures about 50 feet. I place three balls side-by-side using my standard putting stance. Using my IPF, I retract the putter slowly until I visualize 3 inches of retraction. I count "one, two, three," then swing the putter through the ball. The video shows that my first ball travels 24 feet. A second goes 23 feet, 10 inches; the third, 24 feet, 4 inches. My calculation gives me pretty close to an average of 8 feet of travel for each inch of putter retraction.

Next, as demonstrated in the video, I test retraction distance for a composite putt.

Depending on the green practice facility, I like to use a practice distance of at least 60 feet. This distance is not always available at practice facilities.

CHAPTER 6

OVERVIEW

PERSPECTIVES ON
QUANTITATIVE PUTTING

QUANTIFYING THE DISTANCE OF TRAVEL COVERED BY A putted ball for each inch of retraction is similar to quantifying the distance for your other clubs. Most of the time, we find ourselves between clubs and are forced to choose between hitting, for example, a hard 7-iron or an easy 6-iron. As a result, we try to adjust our club retraction, which usually delivers unsatisfactory results, unless we have practiced partial swings with all of our clubs and have them properly gauged. Using a full-swing club to hit the ball your normal swing distance typically results in a better shot for the longer clubs in your bag.

For your short game, you can practice using your pitching, sand, and lob wedges with quarter-, half-, three-quarter, and full swings to cover different distances. Quantitative lag putting employs much the same thinking, the same approach as practicing with your wedges.

There are golfers who seem naturally skilled. But if you analyze their games closely, you will see that their putting skills make their game exceptionally good. Quantifying the method of putting so it's accurate and reproducible improves the putting skills of all players at all levels, from the most proficient to the high handicapper.

ABILITIES REQUIRED TO QUANTITATIVELY PUTT

Let's once again list the simple skills you need to use the quantitative method of putting effectively:

- You must be good at making quick calculations and doing arithmetic in your head as you play.
- You must be able to determine how much distance you cover with your stride, depending on your gait, then be able to multiply the steps you take to determine the total distance you stepped off.
- You should be able to visualize a 12-inch ruler and its increments to make your estimates. The incremental

measurement of an accurate retraction distance is of paramount importance to making this system work for you. The more accurate you become with this skill, the more reproducible your quantitative putting will become.

- You should be able to visualize and estimate a slope of 5 to 45 degrees to establish ascending and descending putting requirements.

- You must determine your own, distinct IPF for delivering force to the ball. Your IPF involves such technical considerations as mass, acceleration, friction, and impulse-momentum. But determining your IPF is a lot simpler; you just have to swing correctly with your shoulders and apply the resulting distances per inch of retraction. Successful quantitative putting is based on understanding the force you require and the frictional resistance of the various surfaces your ball must travel over: for a composite putt, the first cut of rough, fairway surface, fringe, and green.

A DEEPER DIVE INTO IPF

Let's review the critically important and unique constant for each player, namely, your IPF.

Your IPF is the measurement of the force you apply to the golf ball by rocking your shoulders during your putting stroke, along with the retraction distance you remove the putter from the ball before taking your stroke. Because each golfer's individual approach to putting is unique, the IPF varies from golfer to golfer. Your IPF depends on your personal strength inherent in the shoulder rocking motion, the speed of your putter stroke, and the distance of retraction of your putter from the ball.

The consistency of the force applied to the ball by the natural rocking of the shoulders creates a putting stroke that is constant and makes everything function on a linear basis. There is no need to stroke easier or harder for short or long-distance putts; just decrease the putter retraction distance from the ball for shorter distance putts and increase it for long-distance putts on the known and quantified basis of your IPF. The principle is consistent with the laws of physics and engineering mechanics.

Your IPF is also different for each surface, as it represents your normal putting stroke through the ball on a particular surface. Once you establish your IPF for a given surface, whether it is in-home practice, course practice green, or on the course, it will allow you to putt accurately and consistently, regardless of how far away from the hole your ball lies. Many recreational golfers have a tendency to let up or baby the short putt and muscle up on the long putt; both approaches usually end up with disastrous results, either way too short or way too long. Establishing your IPF by using your normal, comfortable, and consistent putting stroke through the ball to determine the right retraction distance provides the accuracy and consistency to make a correct distance putt every time.

The ideal place to develop your IPF is in your house, if you have one or more surfaces of 24 to 36 feet in length to practice 1-, 2- and 3-inch retractions. If this surface is not available in your home, the practice green at your home course is also a good place to develop your IPF.

Loyce and I have two carpeted putting surfaces in our home, and we practice our putting as time permits. In our entertainment room, we have a closely cropped carpet, which we used to establish our respective IPFs. Mine is 11 feet per inch of retraction, and Loyce's is 9 feet per inch. On our more plush carpet in our great room, my IPF is 9 feet per inch of retraction, Loyce's is 7.5. As you will note, there is a linear consistency to our IPF on different putting surfaces, as there is on every golf course we play. But knowing our IPF for any course by establishing it in and around the green practice facility prior to playing the course allows us to play the greens on courses new to us like we've played them before.

A METHOD AND PLAN

Putting by the Numbers does not intend to tell you how to putt but to give you a method and plan for when you are putting. Here's how I go about it:

- I determine how far the ball is from the cup by stepping it off or using my rangefinder.
- I look at the putt from both the ball side and opposing side of the hole on the line of the putt.
- I look at the elevation change from a side view of either an upward or downward slope.
- I plumb-bob the line of the putt with my putter. (Not all golfers buy into plumb-bobbing.)
- If it is a downhill or uphill putt, I imagine how water might flow on that surface.
- I adjust my retraction distance based on the elevation changes.
- I do my quick arithmetic and determine the retraction distance I need to make the putt.

PUTTING FUNDAMENTALS

Quantitative putting as a system does not include requirements for your setup, hand position, location, or posture. But of course, all putting involves some common elements and requires good fundamentals, such as (as described for a right-handed player):

- open stance, leaning left
- ball position off the left toe
- squared putter face
- length of backswing (retraction) to determine the distance of ball travel
- wrist flat and angled the same throughout the stroke
- counting: one, behind the ball; two, retract the putter; three, stroke the putter through the ball

There are numerous putting setup and execution regimens. The quantitative method of putting works for all putting techniques.

THE SHORT PUTT AND MAPPING

Let's examine the role of two putting variables: the short putt resulting from your excellent execution of the quantified lag putt, and the conditions and contours of the putting surface as better defined by mapping.

- The short putt: Note that the diameter of a golf hole is 4.25 inches, and the diameter of a standard golf ball is 1.68 inches. At short distances from the golf hole, say

3 to 5 feet, it is critical to roll the ball on an accurate path. As you can see from the table on page 58, even if the putt is on a level putting surface with no break, it doesn't take much angular movement of the putter face from perpendicular to the axis of ball travel to cause you to miss the putt. It stands to reason that the shorter the retraction of the putter, the more likely you are to keep the putter in a good perpendicular orientation through the ball.

If I have determined that the speed of the green for the day is 20 feet of travel per 1 inch of retraction, and my ball is sitting on a level putting surface 5 feet from the hole, I need only a 1/4-inch retraction to make the ball travel 5 feet. Again, good putters prefer their ball to travel past the hole if they miss, rather than being short. Therefore, trying not to baby the putt, I would strike the ball with a 3/8- to 1/2-inch retraction, knowing that if I were to miss, I would be no more than 5 feet past the hole. Using your consistent putting stroke with your predetermined IPF for the course that day, you are likely to make this putt consistently. In my approach to short putting with a short retraction distance and my consistent stroke, I find that I am rather popping the ball through the stroke with the center of my putter face, without employing more or less power.

Slope and break can make even putts under 5 feet challenging. In these more difficult instances, I reduce my retraction distance for downhill putts and increase it for uphill
putts. I account for the break by picking a target between my
ball and the hole, then establishing the retraction distance
based on the target.

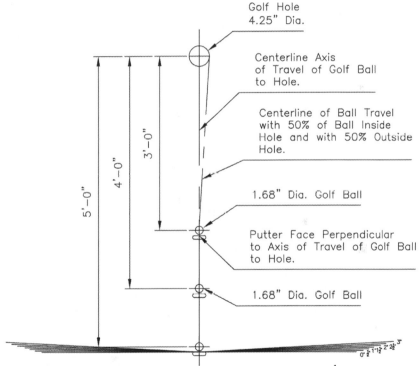

Note: Incrementally, if we rotate the putter face $\frac{1}{2}$ degree
from perpendicular to the axis of travel of the golf ball
the table below shows whether or not you made the putt,
if the center of the ball is more than 0.84" outside
the tangent intersect of the hole. The likelihood of making
the putt goes to zero.

TABLE

DISTANCE BALL FROM HOLE	DEGREES PUTTER FACE REMOVED FROM PERPENDICULAR OF AXIS OF BALL TRAVEL					
	$\frac{1}{2}°$	1°	$1\frac{1}{2}°$	2°	$2\frac{1}{2}°$	3°
	DISTANCE CENTERLINE OF BALL FROM CENTERLINE OF HOLE (IN INCHES)					
3'−0"	0.3132	0.6284	0.9427	1.2571	1.5718	1.8867
4'−0"	0.4176	0.8400	1.2576	1.6752	2.0976	2.5152
5'−0"	0.5220	1.0500	1.5720	2.0940	2.6220	3.1440

NEARLY 100% PROBABILITY OF MAKING THE PUTT.

NEARLY 0% PROBABILITY OF MAKING THE PUTT.

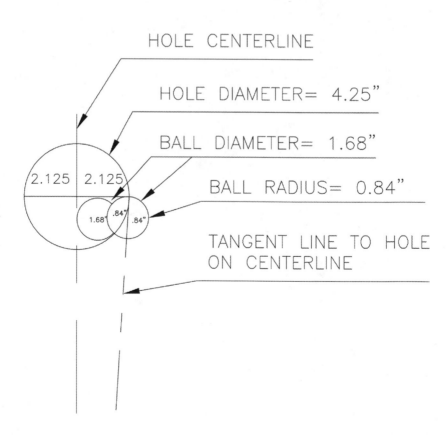

HOLE CENTERLINE

HOLE DIAMETER= 4.25"

BALL DIAMETER= 1.68"

BALL RADIUS= 0.84"

TANGENT LINE TO HOLE ON CENTERLINE

2.125   2.125

1.68"   .84"   .84"

In any event, the retraction distance of the putter should never be more than twice what you calculate to get the ball in the hole. In this way, if you happen to miss, you will wind up no farther away than the putt you just missed.

(Note: There are so many good books on putting, I yield to those experts for their insights on technique and the mental aspects of short putting.)

○ Laser mapping: Amateurs as well as professional players are using the technology of laser mapping to further enhance the accuracy of their putting. About 95 percent of PGA tour professionals and their caddies use green mapping books to enhance their putting routines and execution.

Producers of green mapping books for professional players, like Tour Sherpa, Strackaline, and GolfLogix, keep up with the requirements associated with the setup of the greens each day of tournament play; many of the players and their caddies rely heavily on these mapping books for their approach shots as well as for putting—so much so that, depending on the level of detail, the nature of the information, and the level of the competition, pros will pay thousands of dollars for a tournament mapping book.

Recreational players also use green mapping books, though less customized versions. Even though hole locations are changed regularly, knowing the contours of your home course greens will prove helpful in where to try to land your approach shot and how your lag putt is going to move. Typically, you can buy a green mapping book for your home course for less than a hundred dollars, not a bad investment considering you probably play at least 80 percent of your rounds there. Go to the websites of the green map producers and look up your course for cost and availability.

The USGA and R&A have expressed reservations about the extraordinarily precise information these books are providing to the professional tournament player. They suggest the technology is diluting the fundamental skill level of putting and the challenges associated with the overall play of the game. We might anticipate in the near future the reduced use or total elimination of these books in professional tournament play.

Despite the ongoing improvement in the technology associated with golf, there is still no substitute for being able to apply the proper force to a golf ball in a lag putting situation to get it in the hole or close enough for a makeable short putt.

PRACTICE, PRACTICE, PRACTICE

To get started with quantitative putting, I recommend you practice at least thirty minutes a day, two or three days a week, at home or on your course practice green, to determine your IPF for a given surface. That will help you function with confidence and consistency every time you play and on all course surfaces. At your home or an away course, simply going through the twenty-minute pre-practice regimen on and around the green will prepare you to putt the course with confidence and accuracy.

Initially, a short back swing may feel a bit uncomfortable; it might be quite different from what you are used to doing. But the control and accuracy you derive from this approach will be worth the time you invest in learning it. As you can see in the accompanying videos(Visit: www.puttingbythenumbers.com/tutorials), when I retract the putter to the desired distance, I may have a little waggle in my putter before I strike the ball from the desired distance, but both the distance of retraction and the perpendicular orientation of the putter to the axis of the ball travel are consistent from one putt to the next.

I think we can all remember the first time we held a golf club and were instructed how to properly grip it. That grip was not very intuitive, but after we learned it, it felt uncomfortable to grip the club any other way.

In my personal examples, as provided in the accompanying videos of my practice regimens in my house and at my home club, my IPF is constant at home but changes according to the time of year and the conditions of the greens at the Legends. The speed of the greens during the summer months, when the grass is healthy, cut short, and rolled, typically varies between 10 and 11 on the Stimpmeter. For me, these readings indicate an IPF of 22 to 24 feet per inch of retraction.

EPILOGUE

PUTTING BY THE NUMBERS DELIVERS A METHOD OF LONG-DIS-
tance or lag putting that is accurate and reproducible through
a quantitative method. Many good putters have a natural athletic ability to putt because the "feel and touch" method is
natural to them. But for the more than 90 percent of us who
play golf and do not have that gift, quantitative putting will
save 3 to 5 strokes per round. It is a system you can rely on to
be accurate and reproducible on every putt, an arithmetically
developed plan of attack that works.

Here are some key things to recognize to get the most
success from quantitative putting:

- The ball travel in putting is a friction and force event.
- You can use whatever putting grip you choose and are
  comfortable with, as long as you allow your shoulders
  to create a pendulum swing through the ball.
- When executing the stroke, you do so according to
  your IPF, which is distinctly and individually yours.

- By quickly evaluating the relative slope, the distance, the green, the fringe, or fairway you may be putting from, you arithmetically decide how far you have to retract your putter from the ball for it to travel the right distance to create that inside 3- or 5-foot putt.
- Quantitative putting takes no more time to execute than any other approach since it involves things you already do in evaluating a putt: gauge the uphill or downhill slope, assess the putt from behind the ball, and view it from the opposing direction. The difference is that while you are sizing up your putt, you are also doing the arithmetic to determine how much force you have to apply to overcome the friction associated with your putt.

RECOMMENDED READING

For more information on the putting probabilities from various distances and for various levels of player skill:

- ⛳ www.scottsacket.com/putting-probabilities
- ⛳ www.tomfieldinggolf.net/putting-probabilities.html
- ⛳ www.free-golf-lessons.com/golf-putting
- ⛳ www.golfalot.com/buyingguides/putters.aspx
- ⛳ www.golfwrx.com/
- ⛳ www.PGAdigitalgolfAcademy.com/video
- ⛳ *The Little Book of Putting* by Ian Hardie

PUTTING TURF

Two dominant types of grass are used for putting green construction throughout the world: creeping Bentgrass and Bermuda. Bentgrass is dominant where temperatures are moderate to cool, and Bermuda is the preferred turf in the Southern United States and tropical climates. Bentgrass is used on 79 percent of the greens in the United States, Bermuda on 21 percent. From a survey of over 16,000 courses conducted by the Golf Course Superintendent Association of America:

STATE	PERCENT BENT	PERCENT BERMUDA
FLORIDA	1	99
GEORGIA	48	52
SOUTH CAROLINA	13	87
NORTH CAROLINA	66	34
ALABAMA	18	82
TENNESSEE	64	36
MISSISSIPPI	8	92
LOUISIANA	1	99
TEXAS	50	50
ARIZONA	60	40
OKLAHOMA	90	10
ARKANSAS	60	40
NEVADA	94	6
CALIFORNIA	87	13
HAWAII	0	100

All other states are 100 percent Bentgrass greens.

For more information on the grasses used for putting surfaces:
- www.jacklingolf.com
- https://home.howstuffworks.com/what-type-of-grass-is-used-on-putting-greens.htm

ACKNOWLEDGMENTS

I WANT TO THANK MIKE SHAW, A LIFELONG PROFESSIONAL writer, for his editing and for the pulling together the last chapters of the book so that it is a concise and clear instruction manual for this quantitative method of lag putting. Mike Shaw is an Atlanta-based writer and editor. He counts more than 12,000 published articles, from investigative pieces adopted by 60 Minutes and ABC 20/20 to ghostwritten articles, white papers, and blogs for corporate clients. He has founded and presided over three Atlanta-based marketing agencies. In addition his first novel, The Musician, released by Blue Room Books in June 2021, he co-authored Understanding Economic Equilibrium, published in May 2021 by Business Expert Press.

I want to thank my wife, Loyce, for her continued support of my efforts to develop this putting method over two decades. Her eagerness to adopt it helped us win or place in many couples' scrambles.

I am grateful for all the encouraging friends and fellow golfers over the last two decades who pushed me to write this book. Retiring for the final time has given me the opportunity to get that done. When I send these folks their signed copy of *Putting by the Numbers*, I hope they will find the information in it worth the long wait.

Thanks to Dennis Waldroup, senior design engineer and long-time colleague in my air pollution control businesses, for his help making the book's drawings, tables, graphs, and illustrations. His design skills and dedication are responsible for the quality of those depictions.

Jill and Tim Gray of High Focus Photography of Eureka, Missouri, are responsible for the quality production of the in-home and on-course videos. Jill and Tim devoted countless hours and effort on audio and video to ensure a professional result that clearly and understandably explains quantitative putting.

Printed in the United States
by Baker & Taylor Publisher Services